Backstage Forms

by Paul Carter

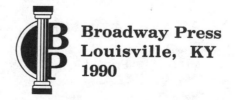
Broadway Press
Louisville, KY
1990

Publisher's Cataloging in Publication
(Prepared by Quality Books Inc.)

Carter,
    Backstage forms / by Paul Carter.
    p. cm.
    6th printing.
    Originally published 1990.
    ISBN 0-911747-35-4

PN2073.C37   792'.02
                               QBI94-21333

ISBN: 0-911747-35-4

For more information about this title, or to request a
complete catalog, please call toll-free, 800-869-6372.

Broadway Press
3001 Springcrest Dr., Louisville, KY 40241-2755
tel: 502-426-1211; fax: 502-423-7467
e-mail: dkr@broadwaypress.com
Web site: http://www.broadwaypress.com

Seventh Printing: May, 1999

Printed in the United States of America

 **Table of Contents**

Table of Contents

Author's Note

Anyone who has spent those endless hours in the theatre recognizes the importance of organization. Without it, a production falls apart: technical rehearsals take days longer than they should; props end up SL instead of SR; and the telephone doesn't ring when it's supposed to. The right forms can solve all these problems. A good form creates order out of chaos, light out of darkness. I have collected as many forms as I could, weeded out the bad ones, adapted the best, and compiled them into this book.

These forms have been collected from a variety of sources - from community, educational, resident and Broadway theatres. There should be a wide enough selection so that you can choose those forms which serve your needs. On the slim chance that you can't find exactly what you need, there are blank forms at the end. Speaking of blanks, the empty space at the top center of each form is provided for your theatre's logo. If you have a favorite form that isn't in this book, please send me a copy c/o Broadway Press and I'll try to incorporate it into the next edition.

The way this book is bound - called perfect binding - is not entirely perfect for the way you will be using the book. We had planned to have a spiral binding, but we changed our minds when we found that the spirals copied just as well as the forms. Loose sheets are more convenient when trying to make copies, but loose sheets are easily lost and they're difficult to package in a way that bookstores will stock them on their shelves. In the end, "perfect binding" turned out to be the least imperfect.

Special thanks to David Rodger and Deborah Hazlett for their invaluable contribution. I would also like to thank those who contributed forms and/or acted as readers: Bill Allison, Anita Bunne, Allan M. Bailey, Mark DiQuinzio & Mary Hayes, Patrick Finelli, Steve Friedlander, Bob Scales, Russ Swift, John Tissot, and of course, L'il Sal.

Paul Carter
New York City
1990

◆ Accident Report

Production: _____

_____

Date: _____

By: _____

Page: _____ of _____

Name of injured worker: _____ Birth date: _____

Social Security No.: _____ Phone: _____

Home address: _____

Name of supervisor: _____

Location where accident occured: _____

Time and date of accident: _____

_____

Description of accident: _____

_____

_____

_____

_____

_____

Description of First Aid given: _____

_____

_____

_____

_____

_____

_____

Signature : _____
(person filling out form)

c.c. to: _____ _____

_____ _____

Crew Call

Production: _____

_____

Date: _____

By: _____

Page: _____ of _____

Name	Time Called	Department / Assignment	Call Length	

Backstage Forms ©

5

Crew Call

Production: _____

_____

Name	Department / Assignment	Call Time						
		M	T	W	T	F	S	S

Crew Call

Production: _____

Week Ending: _____
By: _____
Page: _____ of _____

Name	Department / Assignment	Call Time						
		M	T	W	T	F	S	S

◈ Crew Call

Production: _____

_____

Date: _____

By: _____

Page: _____ of _____

	Name	Department	Hours			Shows	
			Time In	Meal	Time Out	1st	2nd

Drawing Storage

Production: _____

_____

Date: _____

By: _____

Page: _____ of _____

Inventory of drawings	
Sheet no.	Description

Sign out log - Drawing sets

Set	To whom	Date out	Date in	Notes
1				
2				
3				
4				
5				

◈ Employment Application

Production: _____

_____

Name _____
(Please print)   (Last)   (First)   (M.I.)

Address _____

City _____ **State** _____ **Zip** _____

Phone _____ _____
                    (Day)   (Night)

Desired position and occupational goals:

_____

_____

_____

_____

_____

_____

_____

_____

Areas of skill and proficiency in technical theatre:

Put the appropriate number to each area:
1 - Proficient
2 - Competent
3 - Adequate
4 - Interested, inexperienced
5 - No interest

____ Stage Mgt.	____ Wardrobe
____ Grip	____ Costume
____ Carpentry	____ Props
____ Electric	____ Follow spot
____ Sound	____ Fly / Rigging

Availability:
(check one)

☐ **Full Time**   ☐ **Steady Part Time**   ☐ **Occasional**

Describe previous experience and/or educational background:

_____

_____

_____

_____

_____

_____

Former Employers (List most recent employer first)

Date (from - to)	Name & address of employer	Your position	Reason for leaving

References

Name	Occupation	Address	Telephone

I authorize investigation of all statements contained in this application.

Signature _____ Date _____

Interview notes: _____
_____
_____
_____
_____
_____

◈ Employment Contract - Design

Production:_____

_____

This agreement by and between _____, hereafter called the "Theatre,"

and _____, hereafter called the "Designer," pertains to the

production of _____, hereafter known as the "Play."

In consideration of premises and mutual undertakings contained herein, the parties agree:

1. Designer agrees to design _____ for the Play, scheduled to open on

_____ and to close on _____. Unless otherwise specified,

the production will take place at _____ .

2. The Theatre will provide special considerations as follows:

_____

_____

_____

3. The Employee will provide special considerations as follows:

_____

_____

_____

_____

4. The Theatre agrees to pay the Designer the sum of $ _____ ,

to be paid in the following manner:

$_____ upon the signing of this agreement.

$_____ on _____

$_____ on_____

$_____ on Opening Night _____

5. The designer agrees to render such services as is usually associated with the term _____ Designer, including but not limited to:

  A. Providing such renderings, models, drawings, plots, etc. as necessary.

  B. Providing sufficient working drawings for construction purposes, on a schedule as determined by the Theatre.

  C. Designing, selecting or approving all costume accessories or set/prop pieces, as applicable.

  D. To be in residence to supervise construction of costumes or set construction or scene painting, as applicable; to preside over technical rehearsal; to be in residence a total of _____ days, including put-in and technical rehearsal week, through opening night.

6. Designer shall have the right of first refusal to design any subsequent reproduction of the Play when said reproduction is under the control of the Theater.

7. Theatre will not assign, lease, sell, license, or otherwise use, directly or indirectly, any of the designs or costumes or settings, as applicable, for any use whatsoever without prior written approval of Designer and without negotiating with Designer for such use.

8. This contract may be terminated by either party and without cause upon_____ days written notice. If termination is invoked by either party, compensation will be pro rated according to the date of the termination. This contract will be terminated automatically upon expiration of any of the terms of this contract.

We the undersigned, have read the foregoing agreement and do hereby approve and agree to be bound
by the terms thereof.

Signed and agreed to this_____ day of _____.

_____   _____
For the Theatre   Designer

Employment Contract - Staff

Production: _____

_____

This agreement by and between _____, hereafter called the "Theatre"
and _____ , hereafter called the "Employee," will serve as an employment
contract.

1. The Theatre engages the Employee to render services as: _____
_____
_____
_____

2. The Employee will be accountable to _____ for the following responsibilites:
_____
_____
_____

These responsibilities are not exclusive, and the Employee may be requested to perform other duties
from time to time.

3. The Theatre will provide special considerations as follows: _____
_____
_____
_____
_____

4. The Employee will provide special considerations as follows: _____
_____
_____
_____

5. The Employee will receive a salary of _____ per _____ for services rendered. In addition,
the Employee will receive the following benefits: _____
_____
_____
_____
_____
_____

6. The Employee's services under this agreement will commence on _____ ,

and will continue until _____ .

7. This contract may be terminated by either party and without cause upon _____ days written notice. If termination is invoked by either party, compensation will be pro rated according to the date of the termination. This contract will be terminated automatically upon expiration of any of the terms of this contract.

We, the undersigned, have read the foregoing agreement and do hereby approve and agree to be bound by the terms thereof.

_____   _____   _____   _____
For The Theatre   Date   Employee   Date

Pencil Sharpener Use

Production: _____

_____

Date: _____

By: _____

Page: _____ of _____

Date	Brand	No.	Lead Wt.	Color	Initials	Superviser OK

◈ Schedule

Production: _____

_____

Date: _____

By: _____

Page: _____ of _____

Time	Monday	Tuesday	Wednesday	Thursday	Friday	Saturday	Sunday

Schedule

Production: _____

Date: _____
By: _____
Page: _____ of _____

Time	Monday	Tuesday	Wednesday	Thursday	Friday	Saturday	Sunday

Schedule

Production: _____

_____

Date: _____

By: _____

Page: _____ of _____

Schedule

Production: _____

Date: _____

By: _____

Page: _____ of _____

Sign In

Date: _____

Production: _____

By: _____

_____

Page: _____ of _____

	Name and address (please print)	Phone #	Social Security #

Stagedoor Sign In

Production: _____

_____

Name (please print)	Destination	Time In	Time Out	

Telephone Calls

Production: _____

_____

Date: _____

By: _____

Page: _____ of _____

Date	Project	Telephone Number	Person / Company

To Do

Production: _____

To Do	To Phone

Appointments	Other

To Do

Production: _____

_____

Date: _____

By: _____

Page: _____ of _____

Vehicle Sign Out

Production: _____

Vehicle: _____

Date: _____

By: _____

Page: _____ of _____

Name	Date	Time out	Estimated Time in	Actual Time in	Odometer reading

Vehicle Reservation

Vehicle: _____

_____

Date: _____

By: _____

Page: _____ of _____

Time	Block out time needed with your name and purpose / destination						
	M	T	W	T	F	S	S

Work Assignments

Production: _____

_____

Date: _____

By: _____

Page: _____ of _____

Name	Assignment

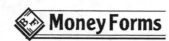

Budget Up Date

Production: _____

By: _____

_____

Page: _____ of _____

Item	Original budget	Actual spent to date	To be spent	Revised budget
Totals ▶				

Cash or Check Request

Production: _____

_____

Date: _____

By: _____

Page: _____ of _____

Name:	

Amount requested: $ ⬜ Cash ⬜ Check

Reason for request:

Charge to account number / project:

Issue check to:

Address (if to be mailed) _____

_____

_____

Approved by:

◈ Invoice

Production: _____

_____

Date: _____

By: _____

Page: _____ of _____

To: _____

_____

_____

Project: _____

For: Services rendered

From: _____ to: _____

By: _____

Description: _____

_____

_____

_____

_____

_____

_____

_____

Total due: _____

Payable upon receipt to: _____

_____

_____

Signature: _____

◈ Labor Estimates

Production: _____

_____

Date: _____

By: _____

Page: _____ of _____

Date	Type of work	No. of people	No. of hours	Total hours	Rate	Total
					$	$
						Total

Notes _____

_____

_____

_____

Petty Cash

Production: _____

_____

Date: _____

By: _____

Page: _____ of _____

Receipt No.	Date	Vendor	Description	Amount	
			Total		
			Cash on hand		
			Total amount of fund		

Signature: _____ Approved by: _____

◆ Petty Cash

Production: _____

_____

Date: _____

By: _____

Page: _____ of _____

Period from: / / to: / /				
Recpt No.	Date	Description of Expense	Amount	

	Amount	
Total this page		
Total previous pages		
Cash advance		
Balance		

Date _____

Signature _____

Approved _____

◈ Phone Estimates

Production: _____

_____

Date: _____

By: _____

Page: _____ of _____

	Vendor	Phone	Contact
1			
2			
3			
4			

Notes

Item	Vendor 1	Vendor 2	Vendor 3	Vendor 4
	$	$	$	$

Time & Cost Worksheet

Production: _____

_____

Date: _____

By: _____

Page: _____ of _____

Item	Time Estimate	Cost Estimate	Time Actual	Cost Actual	Notes
Sub Total					
Contingency (%)			/////	/////	
Total					

Time Sheet

Name: _____
_____

Project	Task	Hours worked							Total
		M	T	W	T	F	S	S	
							Total	

◆ Time Sheet

Name: _____

_____

Date: _____

By: _____

Page: _____ of _____

Date	Time		Hours		Work performed
	In	Out	Reg.	O.T.	

					Rate	Earnings
	Total				Reg.	
		Total			O.T.	
					Total	

Signature _____

Approved by _____

Time Sheet

Name: _____

_____

Date: _____

By: _____

Page: _____ of _____

Week One From: / / **To:** / /

Date	Event	Start	Meals				End	Total Hours	
			Out	In	Out	In			

Week Two From: / / **To:** / /   Total Week One ▶

Date	Event	Start	Meals				End	Total Hours	
			Out	In	Out	In			

Total Week Two ▶

Signature _____   Approved by _____

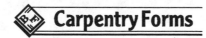

Deck Moves

Production: _____

_____

Date: _____

By: _____

Page: _____ of _____

Scene/Cue	Item	Move

Hampers

Production: _____

_____

Date: _____

By: _____

Page: _____ of _____

Hamper No.	Contents

Hanging Changes

Production: _____

_____

Date: _____

By: _____

Page: _____ of _____

Pipe	Remove	Pipe	Hang

Hanging Schedule

Production: _____

_____

Date: _____

By: _____

Page: _____ of _____

Pipe	Distance	Item	Notes

Hanging Schedule

Production: _____
_____

Pipe	Distance	Item	Pipe	Distance	Item

Rail Cues

Production: _____

_____

Date: _____

By: _____

Page: _____ of _____

Cue	Pipe	In / Out	Speed	Notes

Stock Hang

Production: _____

_____

Date: _____

By: _____

Page: _____ of _____

Pipe	Item	Location on Pipe

Stock Usage

Production: _____

_____

Date: _____

By: _____

Page: _____ of _____

No.	Stock Item	Notes

 **Costume & Make-up Forms**

◆ Bible Card

Production: _____

_____

Date: _____

By: _____

Page: _____ of _____

Character:			Sketch #:		Actor:			
Fabric	**Color**	**Yd'g**	**For**	**Vendor**	**In House**	**Dyer**	**OK'd**
						Out: In:	
						Out: In:	
						Out: In:	
						Out: In:	
						Out: In:	
						Out: In:	

Notes:

Bid Sheet

Production: _____

_____

Date: _____

By: _____

Page: _____ of _____

Character:		Sketch #:			Actor:		
	Estimated Cost			Source	Alter	Combined Costs
	Buy	Build	Rent			
Garments						
Foundations						
Undergarments						
Outer Garments						
Footwear						
Accessories						
Totals						

Breakdown - Female

Production: _____

_____

Date: _____

By: _____

Page: _____ of _____

Actress:			Character:		

Height: _____ **Weight:** _____ **Ring:** _____ **Shoe:** _____ **Hose/Tights:** _____

Dress: _____ **Skirt:** _____ **Sweater:** _____ **Bra:** _____ **Pants:** _____

Pierced Ears: Y_____ N_____ **Allergies:** _____

Requests / Fitting Notes:

Costume No.	Act/Scene	Description	Notes

Breakdown - Female (continued)

Production: _____

_____

Date: _____

By: _____

Actor:		Character:	
Costume No.	**Act/Scene**	**Description**	**Notes**

Breakdown - Male

Production: _____

_____

Date: _____

By: _____

Page: _____ of _____

Actor:		Character:	

Height:	Weight:	Ring:	Shoe:	Hose/Tights:

Suit:	Shirt: /	Pants: /	Sweater:	Trunks:

Allergies:

Requests / Fitting Notes:

Costume No.	Act/Scene	Description	Notes

Breakdown - Male (continued)

Date: _____

Production: _____

By: _____

Page: _____ of _____

Actor:		Character:		
Costume No.	Act/Scene	Description		Notes

Production: _____

_____

Date: _____

By: _____

Page: _____ of _____

Character / Actor:					
No.	Garment / Item	Rent	Buy	Alter	Build	Notes
		$	$	$	$	
	Totals ▸					

Character Log

Production: _____

Date: _____
By: _____
Page: _____ of _____

Character: _____   Sketch #: _____   Designer: _____

Garment	Rented from	Done	Bought from	Done	Altered by	Done	Built by	Done

Backstage Forms ©

◈ Construction Checklist

Production: _____

_____

Date: _____

By: _____

Page: _____ of _____

Actor / Character	Item	Pattern Mock-up	1st Fitting	Sew	Final Fitting	Finishing	Complete

⬗ Cost Breakdown

Production: _____

Date: _____

By: _____

Page: _____ of _____

Character: _____

Sketch #: _____

Designer: _____

Garment	Rented		Bought	Altered	Built
	Fee	Deposit			

Sub Totals ▶

Deposit Total ▶

Total ▶

Costume Plot

Production: _____

Date: _____

By: _____

Page: _____ of _____

Character	Costume changes and variations							
	Scene _____	Scene _____	Scene _____	Scene _____	Scene _____	Scene _____	Scene _____	Scene _____

 **Backstage Forms** ©

Dressing Notes

Production: _____

_____

Character:	Act:	Scene:

Garments	Accessories
	Costume Props

Dressing Notes:

◆ Dressing Notes

Production: _____

_____

Date: _____

By: _____

Page: _____ of _____

Character:	Act :	Scene:

Major Garments

_____
_____
_____
_____
_____

Outerwear	**Hats**

Undergarments & Hosiery | **Footwear**

Wigs | **Jewelry & Accessories**

Dressing Notes

_____
_____
_____
_____
_____
_____

Fitting - Female

Production: _____

_____

Date: _____

By: _____

Page: _____ of _____

Actress:		Phone:		Character:	
Height:	Weight:	Ring:	Shoe:	Hose/Tights:	
Dress:	Skirt:	Blouse:	Bra:	Pants:	

Dress		Pants	
Bust		Girth	
Bust Below		Thigh	
Waist			
Hips		Knee	
		Calf	
Front Neck to Waist		Ankle	
Back Neck to Waist			
Cross Back		Outseam	
		Inseam	
Skirt Length to Knee			
Skirt Length to Floor			
		Accessories	
Sleeve		Head	
Armseye		Hat	
Neck		Glove	
Bicep			
Elbow			
Wrist			

Notes:

◆ Fitting - Male

Production: _____

_____

Date: _____

By: _____

Page: _____ of _____

Actor:		Phone:	Character:		
Height:	Weight:	Ring:	Shoe:		Hose/Tights:
Suit: /	Shirt: /	Pants: /	Sweater:		Hat/Head :

Coat		Trousers	
Sleeve		Waist to Knee	
Chest		Waist to below Knee	
Chest - expanded		Waist to full length	
Waist		Inseam below Knee	
Seat		Inseam full length	
Back length to Waist		Girth	
Back length to Seat		Rise	
Back length to Knee			
Back length to Floor		Waist	
		Seat	
Collar size			
		Thigh	
Vest		Knee	
Open		Below Knee	
Full length		Calf	
		Ankle	
Glove			

Notes:

_____

_____

_____

_____

_____

_____

_____

_____

_____

◆ Fitting - Female

Production: _____
_____

Actor: _____ Phone: _____

Character: _____

Height: _____ Weight: _____

Head - Around: _____

Head - Ear to Ear: _____

Neck: _____

Neck to Waist: F _____ B _____

Underarm to Waist: _____

Shoulder Width: F _____ B _____

Shoulder Seam: F _____ B _____

Shoulder to Bust Point: R _____ L _____

Bust Point to Bust Point: _____

Bust Point to Waist: R _____ L _____

Bust: _____

Underbust: _____

Armseye to Armseye: _____

Armseye: _____

Arm over (bent): _____

Arm under (bent): _____

Sholder to Elbow: _____

Bicep: _____

Wrist: _____

Preferred Hand: _____

Glove: _____

Waist: _____

Hips: _____

Girth: _____

Neck to Floor: F _____ B _____

Waist to Knee: _____

Waist to Floor: _____

Inseam: _____

Rise: _____

Thigh: _____

Above Knee: _____

Below Knee: _____

Calf: _____

Ankle: _____

Shoe: _____

Notes:

Fitting - Male

Production: _____

_____

Date: _____

By: _____

Page: _____ of _____

Actor: _____ Phone: _____

Character: _____ _____

Height: _____ Weight: _____

Head - Around: _____

Head - Ear to Ear: _____

Neck: _____

Neck to Waist: F _____ B _____

Underarm to Waist: _____

Neck to Floor: _____

Underarm to Waist: _____

Shoulder Across: F _____ B _____

Shoulder to Waist: _____

Shoulder Seam: _____

Chest: _____ expanded: _____

Waist to Knee: _____

Waist to Floor: _____

Girth: _____

Inseam: _____

Rise: _____

Waist: _____

Hips: 7" _____ Largest _____

Arm Over (bent): _____

Arm under (bent): _____

Shoulder to Elbow: _____

Armseye to Armseye: _____

Armseye: _____

Bicep: _____

Forearm: _____

Wrist: _____

Preferred Hand: _____

Thigh: _____

Above Knee: _____

Below Knee: _____

Calf: _____

Ankle: _____

Shoe: _____

Notes:

Fitting Notes

Production: _____

_____

Date: _____

By: _____

Page: _____ of _____

| Designer: _____ | Character/Actor: _____ |
| Draper/Tailor: _____ | Phone: _____ |

Item	Alterations/Notes

Fittings Request

Production: _____

_____

Date: _____

By: _____

Page: _____ of _____

Designer: _____

Stage Manager: _____

Fitting Location: _____

Phone: _____

Actor	Date/Time Requested	Amount of Time Needed	Confirmed	Bring to Fitting	Actual Fitting Time

Garment Breakdown

Production: _____
_____

Date: _____
By: _____
Page: _____ of _____

Character:		Actor:	
Act/Scene	Garment		Source/Notes

Garment Log

Production: _____

_____

Date: _____

By: _____

Page: _____ of _____

No.	Garment / Character	Cost				Total
		Rent	Buy	Alter	Build	
Totals ➤						

Maintenance Notes

Production: _____

_____

Date: _____

By: _____

Page: _____ of _____

Character/Actor:					Designer:
Garment	Hot Water Wash	Cold Water Wash	Hand Wash	Dry Clean	Notes / Special Directions

Pulling List

Production: _____

_____

Date: _____

By: _____

Page: _____ of _____

✔	Character	Garment	Sizes	Notes

Rehearsal Clothes

Production: _____

_____

Date: _____

By: _____

Page: _____ of _____

Item Borrowed	Borrowed By	Date Out	Date In

Season Schedule

Production: _____

_____

Date: _____

By: _____

Page: _____ of _____

Production	Designer	Move In	Dress Parade	First Dress	Open	Comments

Season Schedule

Production: _____

Date: _____
By: _____
Page: _____ of _____

Production	Designer / Phone No.	Move In	Dress Parade	1st Dress	Open	Comments

Backstage Forms ©

80

Shopping List

Production: _____

_____

Date: _____

By: _____

Page: _____ of _____

Garment	Materials	Quantity Needed	Unit Cost	Total

Sizes - Female

Production: _____

Date: _____
By: _____
Page: _____ of _____

No.	Actress	Character	Height	Weight	Armpit to waist	Bust	Bra	Waist	Hips	Front of neck to waist	to floor	Waist to ankle	Hat

 Backstage Forms ©

82

Sizes - Male

Production: _____

Date: _____
By: _____
Page: _____ of _____

No.	Actor	Character	Height	Weight	Armpit to waist	Collar	Chest	Waist	Inseam	Outseam	Hat			

 Backstage Forms ©

Source List

Production: _____

_____

Date: _____

By: _____

Page: _____ of _____

Item	Source	Cost	Notes
	Total		

◆ Swatch Sheet

Production: _____

_____

Designer: _____ Draper / Tailor: _____

Character: _____ Sketch #: _____

Fabric	Yardage Required	Yardage Available	Vendor	Dye / Treatment
Garment				
Garment				
Garment				

Wardrobe Sign Out

Production: _____

_____

Date: _____

By: _____

Page: _____ of _____

Character:			Actor:							Dressing Area:		
Item	Performance No. / Date										Strike	
	Out	In	Out	In	Out	In	Out	In	Out	In	Out	In	Cleaned	Vault

Wardrobe Sign Out

Production: _____

Date: _____

By: _____

Page: _____ of _____

Character / Actor: _____

Dressing Area: _____

Item	Performance No. / Date															Strike	
	Out	In	Out	In	Out	In	Out	In	Out	In	Out	In	Out	In	Cleaned	Vault

Backstage Forms ©

Work Assignments

Production: _____

_____

Date: _____

By: _____

Page: _____ of _____

| Name: _____ | Draper ☐ | Dyer ☐ | Crafts ☐ |
| | Tailor ☐ | Milliner ☐ | ____ ☐ |

Character / Actor	Garments	Materials / Supplies / Notes

Date: _____

By: _____

Page: _____ of _____

Character:	Actor:	Script Age:

Designer:

Base	Highlights	Mediums	Lowlights	Hair
Rouge	Lips	Eyes	Body	

Notes: _____

_____

_____

_____

Make-up Work Chart

Production: _____

Date: _____

By: _____

Page: _____ of _____

Actor: _____

Character: _____

Script Age: _____

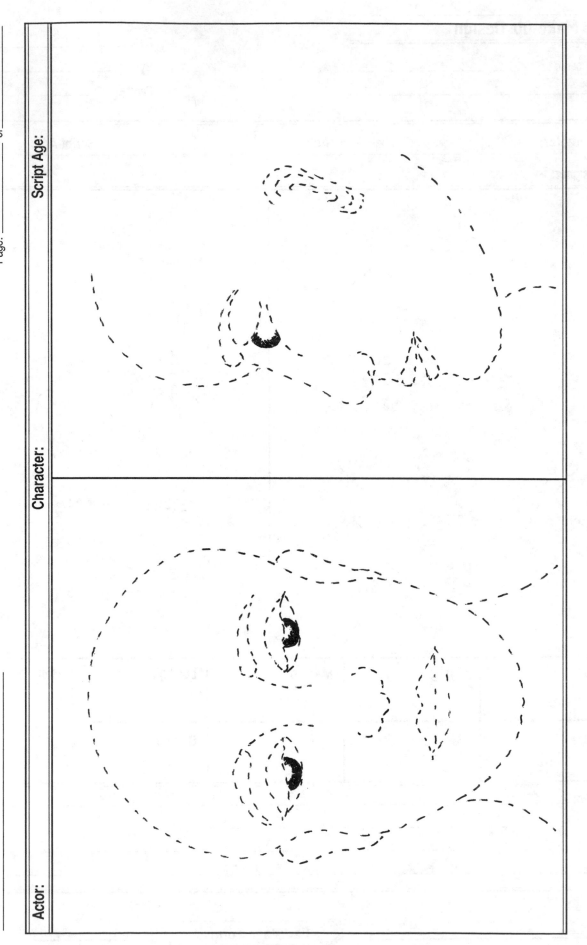

Make-up Worksheet

Production: _____

Date: _____
By: _____
Page: _____ of _____

Actor / Character: _____					Script Age: _____	
Forehead	Eyes	Nose	Cheeks/Jowls	Mouth	Neck	Hair

Area	Color				Application	
Base						
Shadow						
Highlight						
Cheek Color						
Lip Color						
Eye Shadow						
Eye Brows						
Powder						
Prosthesis						

Backstage Forms ©

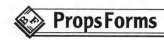

Props Forms

Bid Sheet

Production: _____

Date: _____
By: _____
Page: _____ of _____

Item / Description	Quantity	Estimated Cost			Source	Total
		Buy	Build	Rent		
Totals						

Cost Breakdown

Production: _____

_____

Date: _____

By: _____

Page: _____ of _____

No.	Item	Cost				Total
		Rent	Buy	Build	Stock	
Totals						

Loans and Donations

Date: _____

Production: _____

By: _____

Page: _____ of _____

Theatre / Organization	Donor	
Name:	Name:	
Address:	Address:	
Phone:	Phone:	

Item	Condition	Estimated Value

Terms of Loan / Dates

Received by: _____ Date: _____

Returned by: _____ Date: _____

Prop Breakdown

Production: _____

_____

Date: _____

By: _____

Page: _____ of _____

Designer: _____		Stage Manager: _____	
Prop No.	Description	Act / Scene	Notes

Prop Log

Production: _____

No.	Item	Rent from	✔	Buy from	✔	Build by	✔	Stock	✔

Backstage Forms ©

Prop Plot

Production: _____

Date: _____

By: _____

Page: _____ of _____

No.	Item	SC. ___	SC. ___	SC. ___	SC. ___	SC. ___	SC. ___	SC. ___	SC. ___	SC. ___	SC. ___	SC. ___	SC. ___	SC. ___

 Backstage Forms ©

100

Prop Preset

Production: _____

Date: _____

By: _____

Page: _____ of _____

Preset Location

Backstage Forms ©

Prop Preset

Production: _____

_____

Date: _____

By: _____

Page: _____ of _____

	Stage Left		Stage Right

◇ Prop Preset

Production: _____

_____

Date: _____

By: _____

Page: _____ of _____

Preset Location: _____

_____
_____
_____
_____
_____
_____
_____
_____
_____
_____

Notes: _____

_____

Preset Location: _____

_____
_____
_____
_____
_____
_____
_____
_____
_____
_____

Notes: _____

_____

Prop Request

Production: _____

_____

Date: _____

By: _____

Page: _____ of _____

Item	Quantity	Time / place to be delivered	Date to be returned

Prop Running List

Production: _____

_____

Date: _____

By: _____

Page: _____ of _____

Prop	Starting position	Ending position	Notes

◆ Rental Agreement

Production: _____

_____

Date: _____

By: _____

Page: _____ of _____

Theatre / Organization	Renter
Name:	**Name:**
Address:	**Address:**
Phone:	**Phone:**

Item	Quantity	Deposit	Fee

Terms of rental / dates:

_____

_____

_____

Received by:	Date:
Returned by:	Date:

Rental Log

Production: _____

_____

Date: _____

By: _____

Page: _____ of _____

Item	Source	Quantity	Deposit	Fee
			Total	

N.B. Many of the lighting forms use the terms "circuit," "channel," and/or "memory." As you may know, channel and memory are only applicable if you are using a computerized lighting control board. In modern "dimmer per circuit" systems, the terms "dimmer" and "circuit" are interchangeable. In order not to duplicate all the schedules (one with computer terms and one without) I have assumed that if a certain term is not applicable to your system, you will leave it blank or change it to suit your needs.

◈ Accessory Notes

Production: _____

_____

Date: _____

By: _____

Page: _____ of _____

Cable	Pipe, Bases, Sidearms, etc.
	Color
Frames, Snoots, etc.	
	Dimmers

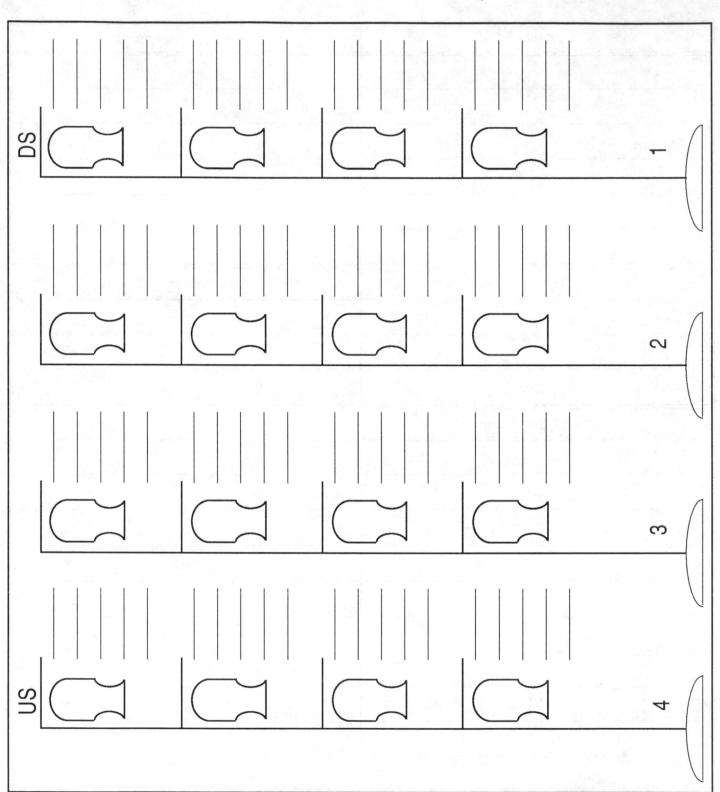

US

4

3

2

DS

1

Channel Hook Up

Production: _____

_____

Date: _____

By: _____

Page: _____ of _____

Channel	Dimmer	Circuit	Position / No.	Type / Watts	Focus	Color

◈ Circuit Schedule

Production: _____

_____

Date: _____

By: _____

Page: _____ of _____

Circuit Number	Position / Number / Use	Circuit Load	Dimmer Number	Dimmer Capacity	Control Channel

Color Cuts

Production: _____

Date: _____
By: _____
Page: _____ of _____

Color	Size	Position									Total

Corrections Checklist

Production: _____

_____

Date: _____

By: _____

Page: _____ of _____

Description	Plot		Cardboards		Hook Up		Cues		Cheat Sheet		Color List	
	Designer	Electrician	Designer	Electrician	Designer	Electrician	Designer	Electrician	Designer	Electrician	Designer	Electrician

Cue Descriptions

Production: _____

_____

Date: _____

By: _____

Page: _____ of _____

Cue	Count	Page	Description

Cue Sheet - Dance

Production: _____

_____

Date: _____

By: _____

Cue	
Count	

Cue	
Count	

Cue	
Count	

Cue	
Count	

Cue	
Count	

Cue	
Count	

Cue Sheet

Production: _____

_____

Date: _____

By: _____

Page: _____ of _____

Cue	Memory	Count	Notes

Cue Sheet

Production: _____

_____

Date: _____

By: _____

Page: _____ of _____

Scene	Cue	Count	Taken On
Page			

1	2	3	4	5	6	Master	Dimmer
							Level
							Repatch
7	8	9	10	11	12	Master	Dimmer
							Level
							Repatch
13	14	15	16	17	18	Master	Dimmer
							Level
							Repatch
19	20	21	22	23	24	Master	Dimmer
							Level
							Repatch

Cue Sheet

Production: _____

_____

Date: _____

By: _____

Page: _____ of _____

Cue	Count	Scene	Taken On	Description

Cue Sheet

Date: _____

Production: _____

By: _____

Page: _____ of _____

Cue:	Taken On: _____		Preset No.
	Description: _____		_____ Manual ☐

	Changes	Tracking		Changes	Tracking
1			19		
2			20		
3			21		
4			22		
5			23		
6			24		
7			25		
8			26		
9			27		
10			28		
11			29		
12			30		
13			31		
14			32		
15			33		
16			34		
17			35		
18			36		

Cue Sheet

Production: _____

Date: _____
By: _____

Action	Time

Deck Changes

Production: _____

_____

Date: _____

By: _____

Page: _____ of _____

Unit / Location	Circuit	Color	Focus

Dimmer Hook Up

Production: _____

_____

Date: _____

By: _____

Page: _____ of _____

Dimmer	Position / Number	Type / Watts	Focus	Color

Dimmer Hook Up

Production: _____

_____

Date: _____

By: _____

Page: _____ of _____

Dimmer	Position / Number	Type / Watts	Focus	Color

Focus Chart

Production: _____

_____

Date: _____

By: _____

Page: _____ of _____

Position:					
Unit No.	Dimmer	Circuit	Focus	Type	Color

Focus Chart

Production: _____

Date: _____

By: _____

Page: _____ of _____

Channel / Dimmer	Unit Number	Focus		Type	Color
Position:					
		S L _____ U S _____ S R _____ D S _____			
		S L _____ U S _____ S R _____ D S _____			
		S L _____ U S _____ S R _____ D S _____			
		S L _____ U S _____ S R _____ D S _____			
		S L _____ U S _____ S R _____ D S _____			
		S L _____ U S _____ S R _____ D S _____			
		S L _____ U S _____ S R _____ D S _____			
		S L _____ U S _____ S R _____ D S _____			
		S L _____ U S _____ S R _____ D S _____			
		S L _____ U S _____ S R _____ D S _____			

Focus Chart - Specials

Production: _____

_____

Date: _____

By: _____

Page: _____ of _____

Unit No.	Dimmer	Circuit	Focus

Follow Spot Cues

Production: _____

_____

Date: _____

By: _____

Page: _____ of _____

Cue	Scene/Pg.	Action	Intensity	Iris	Color	Notes

Follow Spot Cues

Production: _____

_____

Date: _____

By: _____

Page: _____ of _____

Cue	Line / Visual	Spot 1: Action	Inten-sity	Iris	Color	Spot 2: Action	Inten-sity	Iris	Color

Follow Spot Cues

Production: _____

Date: _____

By: _____

Page: _____ of _____

Cue	Line / Visual	Spot 1: Action	Inten-sity	Iris	Color	Spot 2: Action	Inten-sity	Iris	Color	Spot 3: Action	Inten-sity	Iris	Color

 Backstage Forms ©

133

◆ Instrument Schedule

Production: _____

_____

Date: _____

By: _____

Page: _____ of _____

Position	Type / Watts	Color	Focus	Dimmer	Circuit

Instrument Schedule

Production: _____

_____

Date: _____

By: _____

Page: _____ of _____

Position	Type	Color	Focus	Dimmer	Circuit	Notes

Magic Sheet

Production: _____

Magic Sheet

Production: _____

_____

Date: _____

By: _____

Page: _____ of _____

Multicable Breakdown

Production: _____

_____

Date: _____

By: _____

Page: _____ of_____

| Position | No. | Softpatch | Hardpatch | | Watts | Color | Notes |
		Channel	Dimmer	Circuit			

◆ Operator Sheet

Production: _____

_____

Date: _____

By: _____

Page: _____ of _____

Cue	Action	Count	Taken On	Notes

TrackSheet

Production: _____

Date: _____
By: _____
Page: _____ of _____

Cue:	Part:		Time:		Delay:		Profile:		Taken On:	
Follow:							Description:			

1	2	3	4	5	6	7	8	9	10	11	12	13	14	15	16	17	18	19	20	21	22	23	24	25
26	27	28	29	30	31	32	33	34	35	36	37	38	39	40	41	42	43	44	45	46	47	48	49	50
51	52	53	54	55	56	57	58	59	60	61	62	63	64	65	66	67	68	69	70	71	72	73	74	75
76	77	78	79	80	81	82	83	84	85	86	87	88	89	90	91	92	93	94	95	96	97	98	99	100

Backstage Forms ©

TrackSheet

Production: _____

Date: _____
By: _____
Page: _____ of _____

| Cue: | | Part: | | | Time: | | Delay: | | Profile: | | | Taken On: | | |
| Wait: | | | | | | | | | | Description: | | | | |

1	2	3	4	5	6	7	8	9	10	11	12	13	14	15	16	17	18	19	20
21	22	23	24	25	26	27	28	29	30	31	32	33	34	35	36	37	38	39	40
41	42	43	44	45	46	47	48	49	50	51	52	53	54	55	56	57	58	59	60
61	62	63	64	65	66	67	68	69	70	71	72	73	74	75	76	77	78	79	80

 Backstage Forms ©

Sound Cues

Production: _____

_____

Date: _____

By: _____

Page: _____ of _____

Cue No.	Page	Description	Cue Word	Length	Level	Speed

Sound Cues

Production: _____

Date: _____
By: _____
Page: _____ of _____

Cue	Tape		Input				Amp			Notes
	A	B	1	2	3	4	R	C	L	

Sound Set-ups

Production: _____

Band: _____ Set: _____

	Person	Mic. No.	Effects
Lead I			
Lead II			
Backing I			
Backing II			
Backing III			

	Instrument	Channel / Mic. No.	Effects
1			
2			
3			
4			
5			

Notes: _____

_____

_____

Stage Management Forms

LADIES AND GENTLEMEN, MAY I HAVE YOUR ATTENTION PLEASE.

AT THIS _____ 'S PERFORMANCE,

THE ROLE OF _____

WILL BE PERFORMED BY _____ .

THANK YOU.

LADIES AND GENTLEMEN, MAY I HAVE YOUR ATTENTION PLEASE.

WE REGRET THAT _____ IS
(ILL / INDISPOSED / SUFFERING FROM _____).
IN THIS _____ 'S PERFORMANCE THE ROLE OF _____
WILL BE (SUNG / DANCED / PERFORMED) BY _____ .

THANK YOU.

LADIES AND GENTLEMEN, MAY I HAVE YOUR ATTENTION PLEASE.

PLEASE NOTE THE FOLLOWING CHANGES IN THIS _____ 'S PROGRAM:

_____

_____

_____

THANK YOU.

Character Breakdown

Production: _____

_____

Date: _____

By: _____

Page: _____ of _____

Character	SC.___	SC.___	SC.___	SC.___	SC.___	SC.___	SC.___	SC.___	SC.___	SC.___	SC.___

Dance Sheet

Production: _____

_____

Date: _____

By: _____

Page: _____ of _____

Dance Title: _____	Position in program: _____
Choreographer: _____	Running time: _____
Music: _____	
Live: ☐ _____	
Tape: ☐	

Dancer	Phone	Production Notes

Performance Log

Production: _____

_____

Stage Manager:	Scheduled Curtain Time:
Performance No.: of	Actual Curtain Times:

Personnel Reporting Late:

Actors

Scenery

Lights / Sound

Costumes

Props

BF Performance Log

Production: _____

_____

Stage Manager:	Scheduled curtain time:
Performance No.: of	Actual curtain time:

Performance evaluation:

_____

_____

Cast notes	Scene	Start	Stop	Total	Crew notes
_____					_____
_____					_____
_____					_____
_____					_____
_____					_____
_____					_____
_____					_____
_____					_____
_____					_____
_____					_____
_____					_____
					_____

Props	Lights

Sets	Sound

Costumes	

◆ Performance Report

Production: _____

_____

Date: _____

By: _____

Page: _____ of _____

Program	Up	Down	Total
		Total program time ➤	

Weather _____

Cast Changes / Announcements / Problems / Reason for late curtain, etc. _____

_____

_____

_____

_____

_____

Technical Quality _____

_____

_____

Artistic Quality _____

_____

_____

Photo Call

Date: _____

By: _____

Production: _____

Page: _____ of _____

_____

Date :		Time:	Place:	
Photo No.	**Act / Scene**	**Description**	**Actors Required**	

Production Notes

Production: _____

_____

Date: _____

By: _____

Page: _____ of _____

Props	Sets & Lights	Director & SM

Costumes	Sound	Admin. & Misc.

Rehearsal Log

Production: _____

_____

Date: _____

By: _____

Page: _____ of _____

Scheduled Time:		In Attendance:
Actual Time:		
Stage Manager:		
Director:		

Scene	Start	Stop	Total	Scene	Start	Stop	Total	

Props	Lights
Sets	Sound
Costumes	

◇ Rehearsal Log

Production: _____

_____

Date: _____

By: _____

Page: _____ of _____

Rehearsal Time: Begin _____ End _____	
Breaks: Begin _____ End _____ Begin _____ End _____	
Rehearsal detained by:	
Personnel reporting late:	
Run-throughs: Act I	
Act II	
Act III	

Actors

Scenery

Lights

Sound

Costumes

Props

Sign In

Production: _____

_____

Date: _____

By: _____

Page: _____ of _____

Name	Sign In	Dressing Rooms		General Information
		Floor	Room	

Date: _____   **Theatre:** _____

Half Hour: _____   **City:** _____

 **Grids**

Production: _____

Date: _____

By: _____

Page: _____ of _____

Backstage Forms ©